Haiku Guide
to the
Inside Passage

Sally Stiles

PeaCoat Press

Haiku Guide
To the Inside Passage

To Sarah.
A hundred poems
a hundred gifts from the sea
to you with her love

Sally Shiu

4-13-06

For David

from the helm
contemplate this deep channel—
every ripple

This small book takes the reader on a cruise from Puget Sound through the San Juan, Gulf and Alaskan islands. You'll travel the inside passage to Skagway and Glacier Bay, sail into deep fjords, watch wildlife graze remote shores, anchor beside glaciers only accessible by boat or float plane, explore first nation villages and tie up for a night or two at city docks.

It is a record of one particular voyage which my husband, David, and I made from late May to early September, 1998 on our 31-foot Canadian-built Camano trawler, *Haiku*. While David spent the summers of his youth cruising the Northeast on his family's sailboats, and we cruised *Haiku* locally for two summers, this was our first extended cruise together. The story of our trip would not make for a gripping adventure film, for there were no disasters, but it might make for a quietly unfolding love story. Except for ten days when grandson David, not quite fifteen, joined us in Juno, we traveled alone.

Today, there are many definitions of haiku. According to most contemporary scholars, haiku written in English is a very short observation -- a moment of awareness-- written in one to three lines ranging from one syllable up to seventeen or so. Japanese haiku were comprised of seventeen *onji* which translate into twelve or fewer English syllables. Complex, sometimes enigmatic seasonal words are no longer requirements for good haiku. Still, to write a worthy haiku is challenging. With each poem, in as few words as possible, the serious writer of haiku sometimes succeeds but usually strives to:

- Be in the moment
- Be non-judgmental
- Invoke but not express direct emotion
- Create an image that induces contemplation
- Seek *satori* (enlightenment)
- Express the oneness of all in the world
- Practice humility
- Distill a moment through description
- Use simple language, limiting poetic devices
- Limit use of adjectives
- Include an element of surprise
- Juxtapose images
- Utilize one phrase, one fragment
- Tell what, when, where
- Limit gerunds
- Limit personal pronouns
- Be lyrical
- Be truthful
- Avoid rhyming lines

No one haiku does all of this; some of the great ancient haiku break more than one rule. The purpose of this book is to give the reader the gift of some of the haiku moments in this journey and, metaphorically, the life journey we all make.

Haiku is meant to be read slowly, pausing after a page or two. As my friend Michael says: "Collections of haiku should come with something like the pickled ginger which is used to cleanse the palate when eating sushi." The photographs, which David and I took, are meant to serve as the ginger -- places to hesitate, observe and reflect.

echo
down the dock departure day
footsteps, two pairs

I stow *Leaves of Grass*,
watercolors, guitar strings
you recheck the oil

shoreline
disappears from stern
hand tight within hand

gentle wake
laps rocky island
lone cedar nodding

Juan de Fuca Strait
flapping in increasing wind
our foul-weather gear

soup steam rising
draw lopsided heart
on window pane

restless night
a hundred rolled-up charts
tossing next to us

second morning out
water's rhythm becomes ours
blue sky chases fog

look back once more
at Sidney's brilliant sun
toward whitewater turn

run Dodds Narrows
at slack tide
steady boat, captain

Strait of Georgia:
into portlights
saltwater slams

Vancouver:
shadowed by sky scrapers
this haiku

underneath sea legs
white tile floor sinks and rises
city café

summer racing fleet
white mainsails, yellow jibs
jonquils tossed to sea

approach the roar
of Chatterbox Falls
small boat shrinking

in this cove
six hundred miles from home
we are home

deserted shore—
million small ears hear
rotted tree crashing

search for hidden moon:
so many questions for
that old man

mystery to mystery
follow green radar blip
through morning fog

Johnstone Strait:
fighting
fighting sea

waves smash over
shaky wooden dock
smell of bread baking

wrap blanket tighter
write for tomorrow
smooth sea haiku

one-house town
perched on narrow cove
refuge

Sullivan Bay:
washers, dryers, six thin sticks
of celery

in tentative dawn
all the way to Cape Caution
race today's gale

Irresistible,
Searcher, Traveler, Scott Free
fellow ships

swing at anchor
pour a Johnny Walker Black
make tomorrow's ice

low morning clouds
hover over channel
specter ship passes

outside tribal store
main street, New Bella Bella,
puppies – their soft eyes

into dull morning
pod of orcas swim
oatmeal cookies burn

from yellowed shoestring
boy steers red crab float
Hartley Bay

entertain new friends
plastic glasses, cabernet,
yesterday's mulled stew

this June morning
colder than December night
slide back down in bunk

tucked in between
aged fishing boats
Haiku scrubbed so clean

dark night Foggy Bay
still await birthday gift
raise Alaska flag

hang over transom
with knife, mallet, thrashing crab
read instruction book

there squats fogwoman
under Thomas Harbor bridge
calling salmon home

atop twisted hemlock
fledgling eagle appears
wise beyond his days

from deep sea
never again this same sea
ancient fjords rise

narrow channel
seek the surprise
behind each bend

fuel low, water gone
our next boat
Epic Poetry

beg at Yes Bay:
five dollars a gallon
five gallons

Knudsen Cove
dock between two fishing boats
six inches to spare

busy scales
weigh lifetime of stories:
cruise ship charters

after morning swim
mother deer
preens, poses

bear, cub nearby
boater yells to husband
get your sox up, George!

long pine table,
coffee, key lime pie
McFarland's Floatel

winter's work
raffia and pine needle baskets
summer's pocket money

a million drops
a moment's design
thunderstorm

fifty feet of chain,
three hundred feet of line
search muddy bottom

black rock
on rock shore stretches, rises,
sniffs cool air

so many bears
so many eagles
fewer salmon

one by one
ranked down totem pole
frog, eagle, raven, man

reddening sky:
with a gift of halibut
Wrangle fisherman

Elvin shyly asks
if we'd like to tour the town,
gives us his truck keys

Diamond C Café
waitress in tight uniform
everybody's mom

generations past
Tlinglit carved this whale
being carved today

without stopping
over ancient petroglyph
daddy long-legs crawls

square within oval
circle within circle
mystery within

rainy afternoon:
catch starfish and red sculpin
reheat chicken stew

sea lion
out of turbulent rip tide
calmly rising

around bend, Frederick Sound
iceberg slowly glides
glacier becomes sea

swing to and fro
from rock to tilted cedar
dinner theater

school of herring pass
by our dangling hooks
baited with herring

long past bedtime
paint the setting sun:
Independence Day

morning's first light
gill netter drifts
upon gill netter

behind gentle wake
we leave no trace of travel:
deepwater fjord

man and boy talk
flashers, dodgers, salmon lures
man to man

sunny afternoon
boy ascends mountain;
freezing rain, man descends

Sunday sun fades
over western mountain
Monday morning

Haines' streets
thirty years of progress
not much changed

hundred years ago
Soapy Smith murdered
swagger through Skagway

up the gold rush trail
1898 again
follow Chilkoot Jack

beside Dyea river,
once dancehalls and saloons,
iris bloom

at Yukon border
like sourdoughs, dream of Dawson:
mountains yet to climb

humpback rises:
ponder whaling ships,
Ahab's madness

ancestor voices
louder with each beat
Chilkat drums

one man, one woman
meander through creation:
Glacier Bay

written by ice
line after slanted line
earth's history

dodge blue ice bergs,
picture tiny Titanic
tiny band playing

snow patches drift
slowly across jagged cliffs:
alpine goats

midnight, late July
Ursa Major overhead
finally

rugged cabins, bars,
fishing boats and fishing gear
bearded man whistling

Elfin Cove schoolhouse
one blackboard, two erasers,
eleven children

fishing boat quarrel
she runs, face purple-blue
we speak more softly

chain rattles down
tiny spider climbs up
too slowly

a thousand years bridged
in a moment's listening
cedars whispering

lazily we float
alongside sea otters:
Sitka's backwaters

main street, Sitka,
window box geraniums
bent by rain

purse heavy with quarters
laundry, public showers
still ten blocks away

shoreline yellow gouache,
tree trunks watercolor brown
brush stroke, Sitka fawn

nose starting to hook
a stream away from spawning
coho on the line

Exchange Cove fogged in
all day long watch gray
paint over gray

slip into cove
still as time's beginning
await first loon's cry

snuggle down to read
of bears on Murder Cove:
stormy afternoon

Winter Cove:
lean over transom to hear
the calm

Ketchikan Yacht Club
pancake breakfast, sailing talk,
leaving friends

morning mist hovers
just below the treetops
just below the sea

monuments to dead
soar above Alert Bay
bigger than life

facing faces stilled
when potlatches were banned
masks of Alert Bay

duckling in cloud
swallows tufted puffin
now eagle, now bear

morning, nearby shore
sound of one
acorn falling

nine hundred and twelve
to eight hundred ninety-six
summer's cribbage

hide away tonight
watch stars dive into
last of summer sea

mist slowly rises
pull the anchor
one last time

With thanks to
the generous people we met along the way.
To Ashley for all her help.
And thanks to
Ann, Carol, Kira, Michael, Nancy
haiku
my first efforts
your faith

Bill

dawn at Pine Needles
rewrite these haiku
you relight the fire

TJ

winter afternoon
haiku flows quickly
dog warm in my lap

Dalia, Phyllis, Walter, Sena,
Bret, Charlotte
at Vermont College
writers teach writers
generosity

and

with special gratitude to
Aleck, Alastair, Kit, Mac, John, Jug
as my pen slows
your pens quicken:
teacher being taught

*But especially
for David*

page after page
every picture, word
I love you